THE MANIFESTATION PLANNER

THIS PLANNER BELONGS TO:

ISBN: 9781078330527

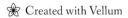 Created with Vellum

"The reason I talk to myself is because
I'm the only one whose answers I accept."
— George Carlin

POST PHOTOS AND VIDEOS OF YOUR PLANNER ON INSTAGRAM OR TIKTOK

AND TAG @REBECCAKSAMPSON

Sign up for the newsletter to receive special offers, mindset resources, behind the scenes of upcoming novels, discounts, and more at

www.rebeccaksampson.com

INCLUDED IN THIS PLANNER

Use special bookmarks or ribbons for the current month, week, and day for easy flipping. All monthly, weekly, and daily pages are grouped together rather than presented with one month of pages in order. This way if you skip a day (or a week) you won't have to worry about messing up the order of your planner.

Between the pages:

- Planner Instructions
- What is the Law of Attraction and Manifestation
- Manifesting Q&A
- Angel Numbers Dictionary
- Your Vivid Vision (2 pgs)
- Your Monthly Plans (3 pgs)
- Your Weekly Actions (12 pgs)
- Daily Intentions (90 pgs)
- Repeat After Me Affirmations (11 pgs)
- Inspirational Quotes (7 pgs)

Use these pages as a companion, not a strict schedule for your to feel shame for missing. That goes against the whole point.

Once you reach the end, go back and review your progress and celebrate how far you've come!

HOW TO USE THIS PLANNER

You are in the driving seat. The driving seat of your life, your thoughts, your manifestations, your life.

The Manifestation Planner is designed to help you see your power, affirm your goals, release shame over your desires, and use the momentum of your daily intentions to create an unstoppable life of your design.

Manifesting your dream reality is not about a to-do list, future-log, or when you are going to the dentist. It is about intentional action and becoming the person you were meant to be.

Whether you are an artist, doctor, stay-at-home parent, author, server, toy designer, or even duchess–this planner is here to help you create change in your life.

Start with the Vivid Vision pages to map out your ideal reality, then break out where to get started in the monthly pages. Your Vivid Vision could be your ideal version of you this year or who you envision yourself to be at the end of your life.

Don't let your Vivid Vision overwhelm you, it's okay if it takes some time to believe you can get there. For now, this will create a guideline for you to begin the monthly, weekly, and daily pages. Speak to your Vivid Vision as if it were you at this moment. Honor the potential of your being and claim it now.

The daily sections were designed so that you can check-in with manifesting amplifiers, like gratitude and self-care, while making intentional choices to bring you closer to the vision. Use it morning and night, but don't worry if you miss a day or two.

Perfection is not the goal. We are here to create some grace, epic manifestations, and a life that you love to experience every day.

Let's start now. Repeat after me: I am unstoppable.

WHAT IS THE LAW OF ATTRACTION AND MANIFESTATION

What you desire is also seeking you. It does not want to feel desperation when it finds you, it wants to feel your peace and certainty.

Imagine this - Your partner left on a vacation and while they were gone you texted daily asking when they were coming back. They answered and gave you updates, yet when they arrived you expressed huge relief as if you didn't believe they were coming. How would your partner feel? Would they want to stay when they felt untrusted?

> Manifestation (*noun*): The act of bringing into reality what you once imagined.
> ie "My book is my favorite manifestation."

In the above scenario, what you were calling in was fear and mistrust. You didn't believe what was told to you, and instead you manifested the person leaving again. You didn't focus on their joy in seeing you, what a great time they were having before coming back to you, or their happiness. Instead, you manifested your fear. You didn't see yourself worthy as being returned too. You found yourself lacking and not worth love.

The law of attraction and other laws of the universe function on your belief, feelings, and faith. The trouble is approaching what we desire with the energy of "want," as that focuses on lack. Lack only brings more lack. Or, when you manifest something that helps your situation, your fear losing it because of that perception of lack, and you manifest a situation that takes it away.

So how can we break this cycle?

Focus on need. You need an overflow of abundance. You need safety and security. You don't want it, you need it. And inevitably, you've had what you needed so far, right? You are here, you have food and shelter, you have clothes on your back, and a pen to put to paper.

It may not feel like you have what you need, but at the core you do. Give the energy of "need" a certainty, because it's the truth. You've had your bare necessities met, so what if you expand your definition of necessities?

You have what you need. And now, take your list of wants and turn them into needs. Have no shame in what you need, even if it's something you would have told yourself before was not that important or even frivolous. Love what you need. Needs are beautiful.

When we break the cycle of lack and shame and embrace what we need, with love for ourselves, because we are worth it, then we bring in more moments to feel certain of our experiences. Through this act, we cultivate more calm certainty.

The world is opening up to you.

MANIFESTING Q&A

Q: What I want isn't here yet. Why?

A: Your ask needs more time to rearrange in the universe. Believe it will come at the right time. If you are asking this question, you don't have faith in it. In some cases, there is a lesson you need to learn before the manifestation arrives so that you can care for what that version of you needs. It is not about having patience, it's about knowing it's still on the way.

If every person that wanted to be a millionaire got the money right away, would they be ready to handle the responsibility that kind of money needs? No. Build the skills you need to receive what you want and it will arrive faster.

Q: I'm saying the affirmations, but I don't feel any better or believe they are true. What do I do?

A: If you feel dishonest saying an affirmation, add an affirmation qualifier. Add statements like:

- I am learning to believe that...
- I am working on my belief in...
- I am in the process of believing that I am...

Adding qualifiers make the statement feel more true. Stay up evidence that your affirmation is proving true and soon you won't need to add the qualifiers. Practice and feel into the energy of your affirmation statements.

Q: I have a lot of negative thoughts. How can I think more positively so I can manifest more positive things in my life?

A: You can still manifest positive events, opportunities, and outcomes even if you have negative thoughts. "High vibes only" is not a sustainable goal. Instead, honor your thoughts, understand where they come from, and release the shame. The key is to grant yourself love and compassion, especially when you feel down, so you can bring in more love and compassion into your life.

ANGEL NUMBERS DICTIONARY

Angel Numbers refer to the phenomenon of your angels and guides sending you messages through number patterns. There are questions surrounding whether or not this is a true path for guidance from angels, but one thing is certain - giving certain numbers meaning is helpful in reprogramming your subconscious mind to see the good all around you.

Below find our interpretation of common number patterns, as told in affirmations. Refer to this page when you see repeating numbers and commit it to memory for daily inspiration and reminders that you are worthy.

Be open to making your own meanings of number patterns. Do you usually see a sequence of numbers when you are thinking of a certain situation or question? Pay attention to what comes up for you and make spotting these numbers a game.

000: *I am open to the opportunities the universe brings me next. The best is yet to come!*

111: *I am a master manifestor. What I want is on the way. I take aligned action to support my manifestations.*

222: *I trust that I am on the right path and all will work out in my favor. I release my worry and embrace certainty in what I desire.*

333: *I am guided! The universe is rearranging to assist me. Magic is unfolding around me.*

444: *I am surrounded by energies of the highest good. I am supported and loved.*

555: *I am ready for the exciting changes coming my way. I take the path my intuition illuminates.*

666: *I invite peace into my life. I realign my thoughts to love and trust the lessons I am about to learn.*

777: *I am lucky. Everything is working out perfectly. I am tapping into my natural gifts.*

888: *I am aligned with the abundance I desire. I am a magnet to money and positive energy flow.*

999: *I am about to unlock my next step because I am clearing up space for it. I release the old and accept the new.*

MY VIVID VISION - IDENTITY

I am

I am

I am

I am

I am

I am

I am

I am

I am

I am

I am

MY VIVID VISION - HABITS

The best version of myself has a life that:

My highest self does these activities regularly:

- -
- -
- -
- -

The person that I am becoming is ecstatic to have accomplished the following based on their identity and habits:

- -
- -
- -
- -

*"Because paper has more patience
than people."*

— Anne Frank

THIS MONTH IS FULL OF OPPORTUNITY

MONTH:

If I could describe the theme of the month in one word or phrase, I would describe it as:

I will take the following actions this month to attract my Vivid Vision:

- -
- -
- -

I am open and ready to receive my hearts desires. Thank you!

This month I will also do these activities just for fun:

- -
- -
- -

Repeat after me: I honor myself by granting myself rest, fun, passion, and joy as often as possible. I am meant to have fun.

THIS MONTH IS FULL OF OPPORTUNITY

MONTH:

If I could describe the theme of the month in one word or phrase, I would describe it as:

I will take the following actions this month to attract my Vivid Vision:

- -
- -
- -

I am open and ready to receive my hearts desires. Thank you!

This month I will also do these activities just for fun:

- -
- -
- -

Repeat after me: I honor myself by granting myself rest, fun, passion, and joy as often as possible. I am meant to have fun.

THIS MONTH IS FULL OF OPPORTUNITY

MONTH:

If I could describe the theme of the month in one word or phrase, I would describe it as:

I will take the following actions this month to attract my Vivid Vision:

- -
- -
- -

I am open and ready to receive my hearts desires. Thank you!

This month I will also do these activities just for fun:

- -
- -
- -

Repeat after me: I honor myself by granting myself rest, fun, passion, and joy as often as possible. I am meant to have fun.

"It is never too late to be
what you might have been."

— George Eliot

THIS WEEK IS AMAZING
WEEK OF:

The top three projects or tasks I will do this week to create my Vivid Vision are:

- -
- -
- -

Repeat After Me: I will use my daily priorities to make these weekly projects and tasks happen, because I trust myself.

This week I am grateful to have the opportunity to:

- -
- -
- -
- -

At the end of the week I will feel:

THIS WEEK IS AMAZING
WEEK OF:

The top three projects or tasks I will do this week to create my Vivid Vision are:

- -
- -
- -

Repeat After Me: I will use my daily priorities to make these weekly projects and tasks happen, because I trust myself.

This week I am grateful to have the opportunity to:

- -
- -
- -
- -

At the end of the week I will feel:

THIS WEEK IS AMAZING
WEEK OF:

The top three projects or tasks I will do this week to create my Vivid Vision are:

- -
- -
- -

Repeat After Me: I will use my daily priorities to make these weekly projects and tasks happen, because I trust myself.

This week I am grateful to have the opportunity to:

- -
- -
- -
- -

At the end of the week I will feel:

THIS WEEK IS AMAZING
WEEK OF:

The top three projects or tasks I will do this week to create my Vivid Vision are:

- -
- -
- -

Repeat After Me: I will use my daily priorities to make these weekly projects and tasks happen, because I trust myself.

This week I am grateful to have the opportunity to:

- -
- -
- -
- -

At the end of the week I will feel:

THIS WEEK IS AMAZING
WEEK OF:

The top three projects or tasks I will do this week to create my Vivid Vision are:

- -
- -
- -

Repeat After Me: I will use my daily priorities to make these weekly projects and tasks happen, because I trust myself.

This week I am grateful to have the opportunity to:

- -
- -
- -
- -

At the end of the week I will feel:

THIS WEEK IS AMAZING
WEEK OF:

The top three projects or tasks I will do this week to create my Vivid Vision are:

- -
- -
- -

Repeat After Me: I will use my daily priorities to make these weekly projects and tasks happen, because I trust myself.

This week I am grateful to have the opportunity to:

- -
- -
- -
- -

At the end of the week I will feel:

THIS WEEK IS AMAZING
WEEK OF:

The top three projects or tasks I will do this week to create my Vivid Vision are:

- -
- -
- -

Repeat After Me: I will use my daily priorities to make these weekly projects and tasks happen, because I trust myself.

This week I am grateful to have the opportunity to:

- -
- -
- -
- -

At the end of the week I will feel:

THIS WEEK IS AMAZING
WEEK OF:

The top three projects or tasks I will do this week to create my Vivid Vision are:

- -
- -
- -

Repeat After Me: I will use my daily priorities to make these weekly projects and tasks happen, because I trust myself.

This week I am grateful to have the opportunity to:

- -
- -
- -
- -

At the end of the week I will feel:

THIS WEEK IS AMAZING
WEEK OF:

The top three projects or tasks I will do this week to create my Vivid Vision are:

- -
- -
- -

Repeat After Me: I will use my daily priorities to make these weekly projects and tasks happen, because I trust myself.

This week I am grateful to have the opportunity to:

- -
- -
- -
- -

At the end of the week I will feel:

THIS WEEK IS AMAZING
WEEK OF:

The top three projects or tasks I will do this week to create my Vivid Vision are:

- -
- -
- -

Repeat After Me: I will use my daily priorities to make these weekly projects and tasks happen, because I trust myself.

This week I am grateful to have the opportunity to:

- -
- -
- -
- -

At the end of the week I will feel:

THIS WEEK IS AMAZING
WEEK OF:

The top three projects or tasks I will do this week to create my Vivid Vision are:

- -
- -
- -

Repeat After Me: I will use my daily priorities to make these weekly projects and tasks happen, because I trust myself.

This week I am grateful to have the opportunity to:

- -
- -
- -
- -

At the end of the week I will feel:

THIS WEEK IS AMAZING

WEEK OF:

The top three projects or tasks I will do this week to create my Vivid Vision are:

- -
- -
- -

Repeat After Me: I will use my daily priorities to make these weekly projects and tasks happen, because I trust myself.

This week I am grateful to have the opportunity to:

- -
- -
- -
- -

At the end of the week I will feel:

REPEAT AFTER ME

I am safe, loved, healed, and happy. I am whole and worthy.

I am

I am

I am

I am

I am

I am

I am

I am

I am

I am

TODAY IS A GOOD DAY

DATE:

Morning Routine

Today I am grateful for:

- -
- -
- -

My top three priorities today are:

- -
- -
- -

Night Routine

I had the inspired idea today to:

One thing I don't want to forget about today is:

TODAY IS A GOOD DAY
DATE:

Morning Routine

Today I am grateful for:

- -
- -
- -

My top three priorities today are:

- -
- -
- -

Night Routine

I had the inspired idea today to:

One thing I don't want to forget about today is:

TODAY IS A GOOD DAY
DATE:

Morning Routine

Today I am grateful for:

- -
- -
- -

My top three priorities today are:

- -
- -
- -

Night Routine

I had the inspired idea today to:

One thing I don't want to forget about today is:

TODAY IS A GOOD DAY

DATE:

Morning Routine

Today I am grateful for:

- -
- -
- -

My top three priorities today are:

- -
- -
- -

Night Routine

I had the inspired idea today to:

One thing I don't want to forget about today is:

TODAY IS A GOOD DAY
DATE:

Morning Routine

Today I am grateful for:

- -
- -
- -

My top three priorities today are:

- -
- -
- -

Night Routine

I had the inspired idea today to:

One thing I don't want to forget about today is:

TODAY IS A GOOD DAY

DATE:

Morning Routine

Today I am grateful for:

- -
- -
- -

My top three priorities today are:

- -
- -
- -

Night Routine

I had the inspired idea today to:

One thing I don't want to forget about today is:

TODAY IS A GOOD DAY

DATE:

Morning Routine

Today I am grateful for:

- -
- -
- -

My top three priorities today are:

- -
- -
- -

Night Routine

I had the inspired idea today to:

One thing I don't want to forget about today is:

TODAY IS A GOOD DAY

DATE:

Morning Routine

Today I am grateful for:

- -
- -
- -

My top three priorities today are:

- -
- -
- -

Night Routine

I had the inspired idea today to:

One thing I don't want to forget about today is:

TODAY IS A GOOD DAY
DATE:

Morning Routine

Today I am grateful for:

- -
- -
- -

My top three priorities today are:

- -
- -
- -

Night Routine

I had the inspired idea today to:

One thing I don't want to forget about today is:

TODAY IS A GOOD DAY

DATE:

Morning Routine

Today I am grateful for:

- -
- -
- -

My top three priorities today are:

- -
- -
- -

Night Routine

I had the inspired idea today to:

One thing I don't want to forget about today is:

TODAY IS A GOOD DAY

DATE:

Morning Routine

Today I am grateful for:

- -
- -
- -

My top three priorities today are:

- -
- -
- -

Night Routine

I had the inspired idea today to:

One thing I don't want to forget about today is:

TODAY IS A GOOD DAY

DATE:

Morning Routine

Today I am grateful for:

- -
- -
- -

My top three priorities today are:

- -
- -
- -

Night Routine

I had the inspired idea today to:

One thing I don't want to forget about today is:

TODAY IS A GOOD DAY

DATE:

Morning Routine

Today I am grateful for:

- -
- -
- -

My top three priorities today are:

- -
- -
- -

Night Routine

I had the inspired idea today to:

One thing I don't want to forget about today is:

TODAY IS A GOOD DAY

DATE:

Morning Routine

Today I am grateful for:

- -
- -
- -

My top three priorities today are:

- -
- -
- -

Night Routine

I had the inspired idea today to:

One thing I don't want to forget about today is:

TODAY IS A GOOD DAY

DATE:

Morning Routine

Today I am grateful for:

- -
- -
- -

My top three priorities today are:

- -
- -
- -

Night Routine

I had the inspired idea today to:

One thing I don't want to forget about today is:

REPEAT AFTER ME

I am a magnet to money. Money loves me and I love money.

I am

I am

I am

I am

I am

I am

I am

I am

I am

I am

TODAY IS A GOOD DAY

DATE:

Morning Routine

Today I am grateful for:

- -
- -
- -

My top three priorities today are:

- -
- -
- -

Night Routine

I had the inspired idea today to:

One thing I don't want to forget about today is:

TODAY IS A GOOD DAY

DATE:

Morning Routine

Today I am grateful for:

- -
- -
- -

My top three priorities today are:

- -
- -
- -

Night Routine

I had the inspired idea today to:

One thing I don't want to forget about today is:

TODAY IS A GOOD DAY

DATE:

Morning Routine

Today I am grateful for:

- -
- -
- -

My top three priorities today are:

- -
- -
- -

Night Routine

I had the inspired idea today to:

One thing I don't want to forget about today is:

TODAY IS A GOOD DAY

DATE:

Morning Routine

Today I am grateful for:

- -
- -
- -

My top three priorities today are:

- -
- -
- -

Night Routine

I had the inspired idea today to:

One thing I don't want to forget about today is:

TODAY IS A GOOD DAY

DATE:

Morning Routine

Today I am grateful for:

- -
- -
- -

My top three priorities today are:

- -
- -
- -

Night Routine

I had the inspired idea today to:

One thing I don't want to forget about today is:

TODAY IS A GOOD DAY

DATE:

Morning Routine

Today I am grateful for:

- -
- -
- -

My top three priorities today are:

- -
- -
- -

Night Routine

I had the inspired idea today to:

One thing I don't want to forget about today is:

TODAY IS A GOOD DAY

DATE:

Morning Routine

Today I am grateful for:

- -
- -
- -

My top three priorities today are:

- -
- -
- -

Night Routine

I had the inspired idea today to:

One thing I don't want to forget about today is:

TODAY IS A GOOD DAY

DATE:

Morning Routine

Today I am grateful for:

- -
- -
- -

My top three priorities today are:

- -
- -
- -

Night Routine

I had the inspired idea today to:

One thing I don't want to forget about today is:

TODAY IS A GOOD DAY

DATE:

Morning Routine

Today I am grateful for:

- -
- -
- -

My top three priorities today are:

- -
- -
- -

Night Routine

I had the inspired idea today to:

One thing I don't want to forget about today is:

REPEAT AFTER ME

I am a magnet to my desires. What I desire also desires me.

I am

I am

I am

I am

I am

I am

I am

I am

I am

I am

TODAY IS A GOOD DAY

DATE:

Morning Routine

Today I am grateful for:

- -
- -
- -

My top three priorities today are:

- -
- -
- -

Night Routine

I had the inspired idea today to:

One thing I don't want to forget about today is:

TODAY IS A GOOD DAY

DATE:

Morning Routine

Today I am grateful for:

- -
- -
- -

My top three priorities today are:

- -
- -
- -

Night Routine

I had the inspired idea today to:

One thing I don't want to forget about today is:

TODAY IS A GOOD DAY

DATE:

Morning Routine

Today I am grateful for:

- -
- -
- -

My top three priorities today are:

- -
- -
- -

Night Routine

I had the inspired idea today to:

One thing I don't want to forget about today is:

TODAY IS A GOOD DAY
DATE:

Morning Routine

Today I am grateful for:

- -
- -
- -

My top three priorities today are:

- -
- -
- -

Night Routine

I had the inspired idea today to:

One thing I don't want to forget about today is:

"To live is the rarest thing in the world.
Most people exist, that is all."

— Oscar Wilde

TODAY IS A GOOD DAY

DATE:

Morning Routine

Today I am grateful for:

- -
- -
- -

My top three priorities today are:

- -
- -
- -

Night Routine

I had the inspired idea today to:

One thing I don't want to forget about today is:

TODAY IS A GOOD DAY

DATE:

Morning Routine

Today I am grateful for:

- -
- -
- -

My top three priorities today are:

- -
- -
- -

Night Routine

I had the inspired idea today to:

One thing I don't want to forget about today is:

TODAY IS A GOOD DAY
DATE:

Morning Routine

Today I am grateful for:

- -
- -
- -

My top three priorities today are:

- -
- -
- -

Night Routine

I had the inspired idea today to:

One thing I don't want to forget about today is:

TODAY IS A GOOD DAY

DATE:

Morning Routine

Today I am grateful for:

- -
- -
- -

My top three priorities today are:

- -
- -
- -

Night Routine

I had the inspired idea today to:

One thing I don't want to forget about today is:

REPEAT AFTER ME

I am influential because I have influence. It is safe to be seen and valued.

I am

I am

I am

I am

I am

I am

I am

I am

I am

I am

TODAY IS A GOOD DAY

DATE:

Morning Routine

Today I am grateful for:

- -
- -
- -

My top three priorities today are:

- -
- -
- -

Night Routine

I had the inspired idea today to:

One thing I don't want to forget about today is:

TODAY IS A GOOD DAY

DATE:

Morning Routine

Today I am grateful for:

- -
- -
- -

My top three priorities today are:

- -
- -
- -

Night Routine

I had the inspired idea today to:

One thing I don't want to forget about today is:

TODAY IS A GOOD DAY
DATE:

Morning Routine

Today I am grateful for:

- -
- -
- -

My top three priorities today are:

- -
- -
- -

Night Routine

I had the inspired idea today to:

One thing I don't want to forget about today is:

TODAY IS A GOOD DAY

DATE:

Morning Routine

Today I am grateful for:

- -
- -
- -

My top three priorities today are:

- -
- -
- -

Night Routine

I had the inspired idea today to:

One thing I don't want to forget about today is:

TODAY IS A GOOD DAY

DATE:

Morning Routine

Today I am grateful for:

- -
- -
- -

My top three priorities today are:

- -
- -
- -

Night Routine

I had the inspired idea today to:

One thing I don't want to forget about today is:

TODAY IS A GOOD DAY
DATE:

Morning Routine

Today I am grateful for:

- -
- -
- -

My top three priorities today are:

- -
- -
- -

Night Routine

I had the inspired idea today to:

One thing I don't want to forget about today is:

TODAY IS A GOOD DAY

DATE:

Morning Routine

Today I am grateful for:

- -
- -
- -

My top three priorities today are:

- -
- -
- -

Night Routine

I had the inspired idea today to:

One thing I don't want to forget about today is:

REPEAT AFTER ME

I am safe to rise to my full potential. I am worthy and capable.

I am

I am

I am

I am

I am

I am

I am

I am

I am

I am

TODAY IS A GOOD DAY

DATE:

Morning Routine

Today I am grateful for:

- -
- -
- -

My top three priorities today are:

- -
- -
- -

Night Routine

I had the inspired idea today to:

One thing I don't want to forget about today is:

TODAY IS A GOOD DAY
DATE:

Morning Routine

Today I am grateful for:

- -
- -
- -

My top three priorities today are:

- -
- -
- -

Night Routine

I had the inspired idea today to:

One thing I don't want to forget about today is:

TODAY IS A GOOD DAY

DATE:

Morning Routine

Today I am grateful for:

- -
- -
- -

My top three priorities today are:

- -
- -
- -

Night Routine

I had the inspired idea today to:

One thing I don't want to forget about today is:

TODAY IS A GOOD DAY
DATE:

Morning Routine

Today I am grateful for:

- -
- -
- -

My top three priorities today are:

- -
- -
- -

Night Routine

I had the inspired idea today to:

One thing I don't want to forget about today is:

TODAY IS A GOOD DAY

DATE:

Morning Routine

Today I am grateful for:

- -
- -
- -

My top three priorities today are:

- -
- -
- -

Night Routine

I had the inspired idea today to:

One thing I don't want to forget about today is:

TODAY IS A GOOD DAY

DATE:

Morning Routine

Today I am grateful for:

- -
- -
- -

My top three priorities today are:

- -
- -
- -

Night Routine

I had the inspired idea today to:

One thing I don't want to forget about today is:

TODAY IS A GOOD DAY

DATE:

Morning Routine

Today I am grateful for:

- -
- -
- -

My top three priorities today are:

- -
- -
- -

Night Routine

I had the inspired idea today to:

One thing I don't want to forget about today is:

TODAY IS A GOOD DAY
DATE:

Morning Routine

Today I am grateful for:

- -
- -
- -

My top three priorities today are:

- -
- -
- -

Night Routine

I had the inspired idea today to:

One thing I don't want to forget about today is:

TODAY IS A GOOD DAY

DATE:

Morning Routine

Today I am grateful for:

- -
- -
- -

My top three priorities today are:

- -
- -
- -

Night Routine

I had the inspired idea today to:

One thing I don't want to forget about today is:

TODAY IS A GOOD DAY

DATE:

Morning Routine

Today I am grateful for:

- -
- -
- -

My top three priorities today are:

- -
- -
- -

Night Routine

I had the inspired idea today to:

One thing I don't want to forget about today is:

REPEAT AFTER ME

I am magnificent. Unironically, I am amazing.

I am

I am

I am

I am

I am

I am

I am

I am

I am

I am

TODAY IS A GOOD DAY

DATE:

Morning Routine

Today I am grateful for:

- -
- -
- -

My top three priorities today are:

- -
- -
- -

Night Routine

I had the inspired idea today to:

One thing I don't want to forget about today is:

TODAY IS A GOOD DAY
DATE:

Morning Routine

Today I am grateful for:

- -
- -
- -

My top three priorities today are:

- -
- -
- -

Night Routine

I had the inspired idea today to:

One thing I don't want to forget about today is:

TODAY IS A GOOD DAY

DATE:

Morning Routine

Today I am grateful for:

- -
- -
- -

My top three priorities today are:

- -
- -
- -

Night Routine

I had the inspired idea today to:

One thing I don't want to forget about today is:

TODAY IS A GOOD DAY
DATE:

Morning Routine

Today I am grateful for:

- -
- -
- -

My top three priorities today are:

- -
- -
- -

Night Routine

I had the inspired idea today to:

One thing I don't want to forget about today is:

TODAY IS A GOOD DAY

DATE:

Morning Routine

Today I am grateful for:

- -
- -
- -

My top three priorities today are:

- -
- -
- -

Night Routine

I had the inspired idea today to:

One thing I don't want to forget about today is:

TODAY IS A GOOD DAY

DATE:

Morning Routine

Today I am grateful for:

- -
- -
- -

My top three priorities today are:

- -
- -
- -

Night Routine

I had the inspired idea today to:

One thing I don't want to forget about today is:

TODAY IS A GOOD DAY
DATE:

Morning Routine

Today I am grateful for:

- -
- -
- -

My top three priorities today are:

- -
- -
- -

Night Routine

I had the inspired idea today to:

One thing I don't want to forget about today is:

TODAY IS A GOOD DAY

DATE:

Morning Routine

Today I am grateful for:

- -
- -
- -

My top three priorities today are:

- -
- -
- -

Night Routine

I had the inspired idea today to:

One thing I don't want to forget about today is:

TODAY IS A GOOD DAY
DATE:

Morning Routine

Today I am grateful for:

- -
- -
- -

My top three priorities today are:

- -
- -
- -

Night Routine

I had the inspired idea today to:

One thing I don't want to forget about today is:

"Our life is what our thoughts make it."

— *Marcus Aurelius*

REPEAT AFTER ME

I am ready for my next level. I am unlimited.

I am

I am

I am

I am

I am

I am

I am

I am

I am

I am

TODAY IS A GOOD DAY
DATE:

Morning Routine

Today I am grateful for:

- -
- -
- -

My top three priorities today are:

- -
- -
- -

Night Routine

I had the inspired idea today to:

One thing I don't want to forget about today is:

TODAY IS A GOOD DAY

DATE:

Morning Routine

Today I am grateful for:

- -
- -
- -

My top three priorities today are:

- -
- -
- -

Night Routine

I had the inspired idea today to:

One thing I don't want to forget about today is:

TODAY IS A GOOD DAY

DATE:

Morning Routine

Today I am grateful for:

- -
- -
- -

My top three priorities today are:

- -
- -
- -

Night Routine

I had the inspired idea today to:

One thing I don't want to forget about today is:

TODAY IS A GOOD DAY
DATE:

Morning Routine

Today I am grateful for:

- -
- -
- -

My top three priorities today are:

- -
- -
- -

Night Routine

I had the inspired idea today to:

One thing I don't want to forget about today is:

TODAY IS A GOOD DAY

DATE:

Morning Routine

Today I am grateful for:

- -
- -
- -

My top three priorities today are:

- -
- -
- -

Night Routine

I had the inspired idea today to:

One thing I don't want to forget about today is:

TODAY IS A GOOD DAY

DATE:

Morning Routine

Today I am grateful for:

- -
- -
- -

My top three priorities today are:

- -
- -
- -

Night Routine

I had the inspired idea today to:

One thing I don't want to forget about today is:

TODAY IS A GOOD DAY

DATE:

Morning Routine

Today I am grateful for:

- -
- -
- -

My top three priorities today are:

- -
- -
- -

Night Routine

I had the inspired idea today to:

One thing I don't want to forget about today is:

TODAY IS A GOOD DAY

DATE:

Morning Routine

Today I am grateful for:

- -
- -
- -

My top three priorities today are:

- -
- -
- -

Night Routine

I had the inspired idea today to:

One thing I don't want to forget about today is:

TODAY IS A GOOD DAY

DATE:

Morning Routine

Today I am grateful for:

- -
- -
- -

My top three priorities today are:

- -
- -
- -

Night Routine

I had the inspired idea today to:

One thing I don't want to forget about today is:

REPEAT AFTER ME

I am worthy of massive compensation, just for being me.

I am

I am

I am

I am

I am

I am

I am

I am

I am

I am

TODAY IS A GOOD DAY

DATE:

Morning Routine

Today I am grateful for:

- -
- -
- -

My top three priorities today are:

- -
- -
- -

Night Routine

I had the inspired idea today to:

One thing I don't want to forget about today is:

TODAY IS A GOOD DAY

DATE:

Morning Routine

Today I am grateful for:

- -
- -
- -

My top three priorities today are:

- -
- -
- -

Night Routine

I had the inspired idea today to:

One thing I don't want to forget about today is:

TODAY IS A GOOD DAY

DATE:

Morning Routine

Today I am grateful for:

- -
- -
- -

My top three priorities today are:

- -
- -
- -

Night Routine

I had the inspired idea today to:

One thing I don't want to forget about today is:

TODAY IS A GOOD DAY

DATE:

Morning Routine

Today I am grateful for:

- -
- -
- -

My top three priorities today are:

- -
- -
- -

Night Routine

I had the inspired idea today to:

One thing I don't want to forget about today is:

TODAY IS A GOOD DAY

DATE:

Morning Routine

Today I am grateful for:

- -
- -
- -

My top three priorities today are:

- -
- -
- -

Night Routine

I had the inspired idea today to:

One thing I don't want to forget about today is:

TODAY IS A GOOD DAY

DATE:

Morning Routine

Today I am grateful for:

- -
- -
- -

My top three priorities today are:

- -
- -
- -

Night Routine

I had the inspired idea today to:

One thing I don't want to forget about today is:

TODAY IS A GOOD DAY
DATE:

Morning Routine

Today I am grateful for:

- -
- -
- -

My top three priorities today are:

- -
- -
- -

Night Routine

I had the inspired idea today to:

One thing I don't want to forget about today is:

TODAY IS A GOOD DAY

DATE:

Morning Routine

Today I am grateful for:

- -
- -
- -

My top three priorities today are:

- -
- -
- -

Night Routine

I had the inspired idea today to:

One thing I don't want to forget about today is:

TODAY IS A GOOD DAY

DATE:

Morning Routine

Today I am grateful for:

- -
- -
- -

My top three priorities today are:

- -
- -
- -

Night Routine

I had the inspired idea today to:

One thing I don't want to forget about today is:

REPEAT AFTER ME

I am stunning. I am stunning. I am stunning.

I am

I am

I am

I am

I am

I am

I am

I am

I am

I am

TODAY IS A GOOD DAY
DATE:

Morning Routine

Today I am grateful for:

- -
- -
- -

My top three priorities today are:

- -
- -
- -

Night Routine

I had the inspired idea today to:

One thing I don't want to forget about today is:

TODAY IS A GOOD DAY

DATE:

Morning Routine

Today I am grateful for:

- -
- -
- -

My top three priorities today are:

- -
- -
- -

Night Routine

I had the inspired idea today to:

One thing I don't want to forget about today is:

TODAY IS A GOOD DAY

DATE:

Morning Routine

Today I am grateful for:

- -
- -
- -

My top three priorities today are:

- -
- -
- -

Night Routine

I had the inspired idea today to:

One thing I don't want to forget about today is:

TODAY IS A GOOD DAY

DATE:

Morning Routine

Today I am grateful for:

- -
- -
- -

My top three priorities today are:

- -
- -
- -

Night Routine

I had the inspired idea today to:

One thing I don't want to forget about today is:

TODAY IS A GOOD DAY

DATE:

Morning Routine

Today I am grateful for:

- -
- -
- -

My top three priorities today are:

- -
- -
- -

Night Routine

I had the inspired idea today to:

One thing I don't want to forget about today is:

TODAY IS A GOOD DAY
DATE:

Morning Routine

Today I am grateful for:

- -
- -
- -

My top three priorities today are:

- -
- -
- -

Night Routine

I had the inspired idea today to:

One thing I don't want to forget about today is:

TODAY IS A GOOD DAY

DATE:

Morning Routine

Today I am grateful for:

- -
- -
- -

My top three priorities today are:

- -
- -
- -

Night Routine

I had the inspired idea today to:

One thing I don't want to forget about today is:

TODAY IS A GOOD DAY

DATE:

Morning Routine

Today I am grateful for:

- -
- -
- -

My top three priorities today are:

- -
- -
- -

Night Routine

I had the inspired idea today to:

One thing I don't want to forget about today is:

TODAY IS A GOOD DAY

DATE:

Morning Routine

Today I am grateful for:

- -
- -
- -

My top three priorities today are:

- -
- -
- -

Night Routine

I had the inspired idea today to:

One thing I don't want to forget about today is:

TODAY IS A GOOD DAY

DATE:

Morning Routine

Today I am grateful for:

- -
- -
- -

My top three priorities today are:

- -
- -
- -

Night Routine

I had the inspired idea today to:

One thing I don't want to forget about today is:

TODAY IS A GOOD DAY

DATE:

Morning Routine

Today I am grateful for:

- -
- -
- -

My top three priorities today are:

- -
- -
- -

Night Routine

I had the inspired idea today to:

One thing I don't want to forget about today is:

TODAY IS A GOOD DAY
DATE:

Morning Routine

Today I am grateful for:

- -
- -
- -

My top three priorities today are:

- -
- -
- -

Night Routine

I had the inspired idea today to:

One thing I don't want to forget about today is:

"Only he who attempts the absurd
is capable of achieving the impossible."

— Miguel de Unamuno

TODAY IS A GOOD DAY

DATE:

Morning Routine

Today I am grateful for:

- -
- -
- -

My top three priorities today are:

- -
- -
- -

Night Routine

I had the inspired idea today to:

One thing I don't want to forget about today is:

TODAY IS A GOOD DAY

DATE:

Morning Routine

Today I am grateful for:

- -
- -
- -

My top three priorities today are:

- -
- -
- -

Night Routine

I had the inspired idea today to:

One thing I don't want to forget about today is:

TODAY IS A GOOD DAY

DATE:

Morning Routine

Today I am grateful for:

- -
- -
- -

My top three priorities today are:

- -
- -
- -

Night Routine

I had the inspired idea today to:

One thing I don't want to forget about today is:

TODAY IS A GOOD DAY

DATE:

Morning Routine

Today I am grateful for:

- -
- -
- -

My top three priorities today are:

- -
- -
- -

Night Routine

I had the inspired idea today to:

One thing I don't want to forget about today is:

TODAY IS A GOOD DAY

DATE:

Morning Routine

Today I am grateful for:

- -
- -
- -

My top three priorities today are:

- -
- -
- -

Night Routine

I had the inspired idea today to:

One thing I don't want to forget about today is:

TODAY IS A GOOD DAY

DATE:

Morning Routine

Today I am grateful for:

- -
- -
- -

My top three priorities today are:

- -
- -
- -

Night Routine

I had the inspired idea today to:

One thing I don't want to forget about today is:

REPEAT AFTER ME

I am in the middle of a big change. I'm open to the magic of it.

I am

I am

I am

I am

I am

I am

I am

I am

I am

I am

TODAY IS A GOOD DAY
DATE:

Morning Routine

Today I am grateful for:

- -
- -
- -

My top three priorities today are:

- -
- -
- -

Night Routine

I had the inspired idea today to:

One thing I don't want to forget about today is:

TODAY IS A GOOD DAY

DATE:

Morning Routine

Today I am grateful for:

- -
- -
- -

My top three priorities today are:

- -
- -
- -

Night Routine

I had the inspired idea today to:

One thing I don't want to forget about today is:

TODAY IS A GOOD DAY

DATE:

Morning Routine

Today I am grateful for:

- -
- -
- -

My top three priorities today are:

- -
- -
- -

Night Routine

I had the inspired idea today to:

One thing I don't want to forget about today is:

TODAY IS A GOOD DAY

DATE:

Morning Routine

Today I am grateful for:

- -
- -
- -

My top three priorities today are:

- -
- -
- -

Night Routine

I had the inspired idea today to:

One thing I don't want to forget about today is:

TODAY IS A GOOD DAY

DATE:

Morning Routine

Today I am grateful for:

- -
- -
- -

My top three priorities today are:

- -
- -
- -

Night Routine

I had the inspired idea today to:

One thing I don't want to forget about today is:

TODAY IS A GOOD DAY

DATE:

Morning Routine

Today I am grateful for:

- -
- -
- -

My top three priorities today are:

- -
- -
- -

Night Routine

I had the inspired idea today to:

One thing I don't want to forget about today is:

TODAY IS A GOOD DAY

DATE:

Morning Routine

Today I am grateful for:

- -
- -
- -

My top three priorities today are:

- -
- -
- -

Night Routine

I had the inspired idea today to:

One thing I don't want to forget about today is:

TODAY IS A GOOD DAY

DATE:

Morning Routine

Today I am grateful for:

- -
- -
- -

My top three priorities today are:

- -
- -
- -

Night Routine

I had the inspired idea today to:

One thing I don't want to forget about today is:

TODAY IS A GOOD DAY

DATE:

Morning Routine

Today I am grateful for:

- -
- -
- -

My top three priorities today are:

- -
- -
- -

Night Routine

I had the inspired idea today to:

One thing I don't want to forget about today is:

TODAY IS A GOOD DAY

DATE:

Morning Routine

Today I am grateful for:

- -
- -
- -

My top three priorities today are:

- -
- -
- -

Night Routine

I had the inspired idea today to:

One thing I don't want to forget about today is:

TODAY IS A GOOD DAY

DATE:

Morning Routine

Today I am grateful for:

- -
- -
- -

My top three priorities today are:

- -
- -
- -

Night Routine

I had the inspired idea today to:

One thing I don't want to forget about today is:

TODAY IS A GOOD DAY

DATE:

Morning Routine

Today I am grateful for:

- -
- -
- -

My top three priorities today are:

- -
- -
- -

Night Routine

I had the inspired idea today to:

One thing I don't want to forget about today is:

REPEAT AFTER ME

I am trustworthy. I trust myself without hesitation.

I am

I am

I am

I am

I am

I am

I am

I am

I am

I am

TODAY IS A GOOD DAY

DATE:

Morning Routine

Today I am grateful for:

- -
- -
- -

My top three priorities today are:

- -
- -
- -

Night Routine

I had the inspired idea today to:

One thing I don't want to forget about today is:

TODAY IS A GOOD DAY

DATE:

Morning Routine

Today I am grateful for:

- -
- -
- -

My top three priorities today are:

- -
- -
- -

Night Routine

I had the inspired idea today to:

One thing I don't want to forget about today is:

TODAY IS A GOOD DAY

DATE:

Morning Routine

Today I am grateful for:

- -
- -
- -

My top three priorities today are:

- -
- -
- -

Night Routine

I had the inspired idea today to:

One thing I don't want to forget about today is:

TODAY IS A GOOD DAY

DATE:

Morning Routine

Today I am grateful for:

- -
- -
- -

My top three priorities today are:

- -
- -
- -

Night Routine

I had the inspired idea today to:

One thing I don't want to forget about today is:

TODAY IS A GOOD DAY

DATE:

Morning Routine

Today I am grateful for:

- -
- -
- -

My top three priorities today are:

- -
- -
- -

Night Routine

I had the inspired idea today to:

One thing I don't want to forget about today is:

TODAY IS A GOOD DAY

DATE:

Morning Routine

Today I am grateful for:

- -
- -
- -

My top three priorities today are:

- -
- -
- -

Night Routine

I had the inspired idea today to:

One thing I don't want to forget about today is:

TODAY IS A GOOD DAY

DATE:

Morning Routine

Today I am grateful for:

- -
- -
- -

My top three priorities today are:

- -
- -
- -

Night Routine

I had the inspired idea today to:

One thing I don't want to forget about today is:

TODAY IS A GOOD DAY

DATE:

Morning Routine

Today I am grateful for:

- -
- -
- -

My top three priorities today are:

- -
- -
- -

Night Routine

I had the inspired idea today to:

One thing I don't want to forget about today is:

TODAY IS A GOOD DAY

DATE:

Morning Routine

Today I am grateful for:

- -
- -
- -

My top three priorities today are:

- -
- -
- -

Night Routine

I had the inspired idea today to:

One thing I don't want to forget about today is:

TODAY IS A GOOD DAY
DATE:

Morning Routine

Today I am grateful for:

- -
- -
- -

My top three priorities today are:

- -
- -
- -

Night Routine

I had the inspired idea today to:

One thing I don't want to forget about today is:

TODAY IS A GOOD DAY
DATE:

Morning Routine

Today I am grateful for:

- -
- -
- -

My top three priorities today are:

- -
- -
- -

Night Routine

I had the inspired idea today to:

One thing I don't want to forget about today is:

TODAY IS A GOOD DAY

DATE:

Morning Routine

Today I am grateful for:

- -
- -
- -

My top three priorities today are:

- -
- -
- -

Night Routine

I had the inspired idea today to:

One thing I don't want to forget about today is:

*"You will never be able to escape from your heart.
So it's better to listen to what it has to say."*

— *Paulo Coelho*

I LEAD AN UNSTOPPABLE LIFE

I have created so much these past 90 days. I am proud of myself, who I am right now, but also who I am becoming.

These amazing things would not have happened if I didn't spend intentional time on myself and understood the power of creating a Vivid Vision of who I aim to be.

The accomplishments I am the most proud of from the past 90-days are:

- -
- -
- -
- -

There was also so much to be grateful for in the past 90-days, like:

- -
- -
- -
- -

I am just beginning. I am unstoppable.

REVIEW THIS PLANNER

Please consider leaving a review on Amazon for
The Manifestation Planner.

Reviews help authors and creators gain visibility.
Bonus points if you share a photo or video in your review.

Thank you so much for your time!

As a thank you for your honest feedback, email me at
contact@rebeccaksampson.com with a screenshot of your
review to redeem a free bookmark.

ALSO BY REBECCA K. SAMPSON

FICTION

The Fated Tales Series:

Ember Dragon Daughter

Hasley Fateless

Ember Dragon Savior (Coming Soon)

NONFICTION

Stronger Now: How to Thrive in Any Circumstance and Become Unstoppable

JOURNALS & PLANNERS

Becky Olivia Journals

The Manifestation Planner

Time to Manifest Journal

ABOUT THE AUTHOR

Rebecca K. Sampson is an author and creative professional living in South Florida with her high school sweetheart and their son. To have Rebecca speak on your podcast or attend a local or virtual event, reach out using the contact form on rebeccaksampson.com.

She writes bestselling YA fantasy novels that help readers take on scenarios that can seem insurmountable like swift change, massive responsibility, and being different through the backdrop of fantastical situations and flawed characters. Her nonfiction work helps multipassionate women like her become unstoppable.

Rebecca loves to journal, stare at the moon, take personality tests, and name inanimate objects. If you'd like to chat on social, you can find her @RebeccaKSampson on Instagram and TikTok.

facebook.com/rebeccaksampson
twitter.com/rebeccaksampson
instagram.com/rebeccaksampson

GET EXCLUSIVE UPDATES

Sign up for the newsletter to receive special offers, mindset resources, behind the scenes of upcoming novels, discounts, and more at

www.rebeccaksampson.com

Made in the USA
Coppell, TX
05 December 2022